Dinosaurs

Tyrannosaurus rex

Daniel Nunn

www.heinemann.co.uk/library
Visit our website to find out more information about Heinemann Library books.

To order:

Phone 44 (0) 1865 888066
Send a fax to 44 (0) 1865 314091

Visit the Heinemann Bookshop at www.heinemann.co.uk/library to browse our catalogue and order online.

First published in Great Britain by Heinemann Library, Halley Court, Jordan Hill, Oxford OX2 8EJ, part of Harcourt Education. Heinemann is a registered trademark of Harcourt Education Ltd.

Editorial: Daniel Nunn and Rachel Howells
Illustrations: Maureen and Gordon Gray, James Field of Simon Girling and Associates
Design: Joanna Hinton-Malivoire
Picture research: Erica Newbery
Production: Duncan Gilbert

Printed and bound in China by South China Printing Co. Ltd.

10-digit ISBN 0 4311 8446 1
13-digit ISBN 978 0 4311 8446 3

11 10 09 08
10 9 8 7 6 5 4 3 2

British Library Cataloguing in Publication Data
Nunn, Daniel
Tyrannosaurus–rex. – (Dinosaurs)
567.9′129
A full catalogue record for this book is available from the British Library.

Acknowledgements
The publishers would like to thank the following for permission to reproduce photographs: Alamy pp. 11 (Mike Danton), 22 (www.white-windmill.co.uk); Corbis pp. 7 (Zefa/Peter Adams), 9 and 23 (Royalty-Free); 16 (Charles Platiau/Reuters), 19, 22 and 23 (Philip Gould), 21 (Craig Lovell); Istock p. 20 (DoctorBass); Science Photo Library pp. 9 (Mark Garlick), 18 (Carlos Goldin).

Cover photograph of Tyrannosaurus rex reproduced with permission of Alamy/Mike Danton.

Every effort has been made to contact copyright holders of any material reproduced in this book. Any omissions will be rectified in subsequent printings if notice is given to the publishers.

Contents

The dinosaurs

Dinosaurs were reptiles.

Dinosaurs lived long ago.

Tyrannosaurus rex was a dinosaur.
Tyrannosaurus rex lived long ago.

Today there are no
Tyrannosaurus rex.

Some dinosaurs were small.

But Tyrannosaurus rex was big.

Tyrannosaurus rex had strong back legs.

Tyrannosaurus rex walked on two feet.

Tyrannosaurus rex had short arms.

Tyrannosaurus rex had a long tail.

Tyrannosaurus rex had sharp teeth.

Tyrannosaurus rex had strong jaws.

Tyrannosaurus rex had a very big head.

Tyrannosaurus rex ate
other dinosaurs.

How do we know?

Scientists have found fossils of Tyrannosaurus rex.

Fossils are the bones of animals which have turned to rock.

Fossils show us the outline
of the dinosaur.

Fossils tell us what Tyrannosaurus rex was like.

Fossil quiz

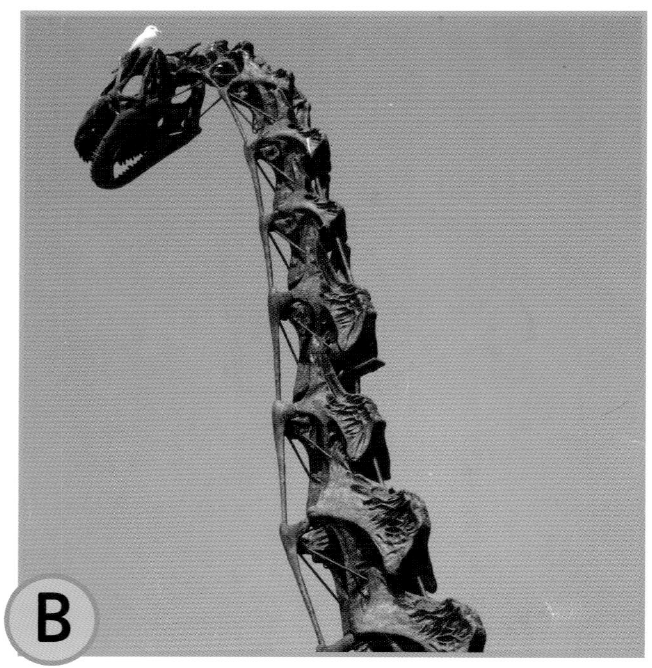

One of these fossils was Tyrannosaurus rex. Can you tell which one?

Picture glossary

dinosaur a reptile who lived millions of years ago

fossil part of a dead plant or animal that has become hard like rock

reptile a cold-blooded animal

Answer to question on page 22

Fossil A was Tyrannosaurus rex.
Fossil B was Brachiosaurus.

Index

Note to Parents and Teachers
Before reading
Talk to the children about dinosaurs. Do they know the names of any dinosaurs? What features did they have e.g. long neck, bony plates, sharp teeth? Has anyone seen a dinosaur fossil or model in a museum?

After reading

- Dinosaur footprints
  Outside draw large dinosaur footprints in playground chalks. Tell the children to move around the footprints using different dinosaur movements. When you call out "Stop" also call out a number. The children should have to quickly stand in groups of that number on the footprints.
- Make a Tyrannosaurus head
  Give each child a lump of clay. Show them the pictures of Tyrannosaurus head and ask them to make a model head from the clay. When it is dry they could paint the head, colouring some of the teeth red to represent the blood of the animal it has attacked.
- Dinosaur poem.
  Ask the children to suggest some descriptions of the dinosaurs and link these together to make a simple poem e.g. Hungry dinosaurs, Hunting dinosaurs, Down in the swamp.

Titles in the *Dinosaurs* series include:

Hardback 978-0431184500

Hardback 978-0431184517

Hardback 978-0431184494

Hardback 978-0431184470

Hardback 978-0431184463

Hardback 978-0431184487